Presented to
Harry

on our Pearl Anniversary
27th September 1999
from his loving wife
Margaret

see 132 for your grandmother's house

SIDCUP
A Pictorial History

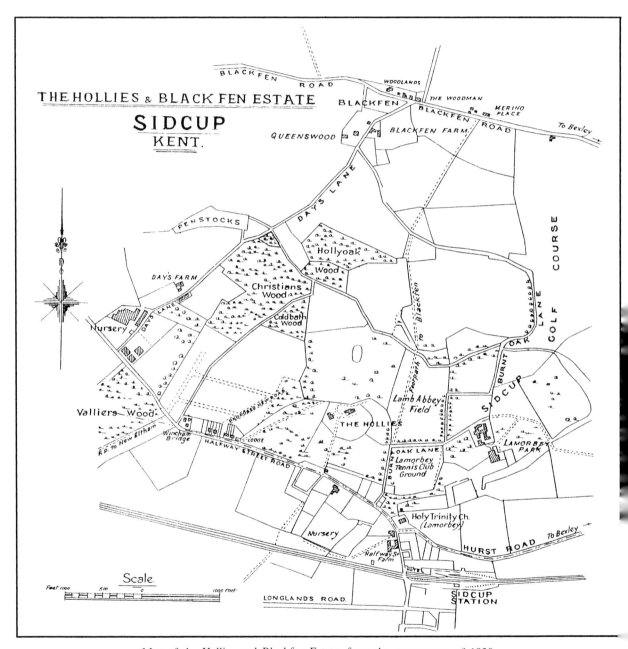

Map of the Hollies and Blackfen Estate, from the conveyance of 1930.

SIDCUP
A Pictorial History

John Mercer

Phillimore

1994

Published by
PHILLIMORE & CO. LTD.,
Shopwyke Manor Barn, Chichester, West Sussex

ISBN 0 85033 907 3

Printed and bound in Great Britain by
BIDDLES LTD.
Guildford, Surrey

To Joan Frances
1925-1990

List of Illustrations

Frontispiece: The Hollies & Black Fen Estate, 1930

Old Maps

1.   Pike Place, Foots Cray in 1683
2.   Estate map of Lamorbey House, 1761
3.   The parish of St John the Evangelist
      *c.*1886
4.   Sidcup in 1869
5.   Foots Cray Village, *c.*1935

Stately Homes and Old Houses

6.   Frognal House
7.   Queen's Hospital in 1917
8.   North Cray Place, *c.*1782
9.   North Cray Cottage
10-13.   Foots Cray Place
14.   The Five Arches Bridge over the Cray
15.   Vale Mascal near the River Cray
16 & 17.   Lamorbey House
18.   The coach house of Lamorbey House
19.   Sidcup Place
20.   'Tudor Cottage' in Halfway Street
21.   The Hollies house in 1986
22 & 23.   The North Cray Hall House
24.   The Old House, Church Road, Foots
      Cray
25.   Queen Anne three-storey houses
26.   Tudor Cottages, Foots Cray High
      Street, *c.*1923
27.   Walnut Tree Cottage, Sidcup Hill
28.   Church Cottage, Church Road, Foots
      Cray

Churches and Chapels

29 & 30.   St James', North Cray
31 & 32.   All Saints, Foots Cray, *c.*1909
33 & 34.   St John the Evangelist
35.   The Rev. T. C. Lewis
36 & 37.   St John the Evangelist
38.   The Rev. C. E. Shirley Woolmer
39 & 40.   St John the Evangelist
41.   A procession on its way to St John's,
      *c.*1907
42 & 43.   Holy Trinity, Lamorbey
44.   The iron church in Chislehurst Road
45.   Christ church, Main Road.
46.   The Congregational church, Station
      Road
47.   The Methodist church, between Hadlow
      Road and Granville Road
48.   Sidcup Baptist chapel in Hatherley Road,
      in the early 1920s

The Railway

49.   A train pulling into Sidcup station in the
      1890s
50.   Sidcup station, *c.*1900
51.   Sidcup station approach, 1920s
52.   Waring Park, 1930s

The Fire Service

53.   The Sidcup Fire Brigade
54.   A fire tender
55.   The rear of the fire station in Main Road

Farming and Country Pursuits

56-58.   Hop pickers
59.   Holly Park Farmhouse, Halfway Street
60.   Hop pickers at Longmeadow Road
61.   Hay making in the 1920s
62.   Picking watercress in 1938
63.   La Retraite Nursery in Blackfen in the
      1930s
64.   The old Golf Glub Pavilion off Church
      Avenue
65.   The old golf links in 1905
66.   The new Golf House off Hurst Road in
      1915
67.   The oast houses at Hurst Farm in 1949
68.   Raspberry picking in the Blackfen area,
      1930s
69.   4 Glen Cottages, Blackfen, early 1920s
70.   Doug Holland's forge at Cross Road
71.   Smokey Joe
72.   The Old Folks at Home

Hospitals

73-79.   The Queen's Hospital
80.   Sidcup Cottage Hospital, *c.*1900

Schools

81.   Sidcup National School in Birkbeck
      Road
82.   The Birkbeck School, Alma Road

83. St Joseph's Convent in Hatherley Road
84. Children from Birkbeck National School in 1904
85. Sidcup Hill School, *c.*1910
86-89. The High School for Girls at the corner of Station and Victoria Road
90. A group of school girls in the 1900s
91. Foots Cray National School in Church Road, *c.*1900
92. The second Lamorbey National School in Hurst Road
93-95. 'The Hollies', Burnt Oak Lane
96. Sidcup Hill School, *c.*1920
97. Staff at Blackfen Secondary School in 1953
98. Hurstmere School, Hurst Road in 1955-6
99. Two Hurstmere boys in 1958
100. Cottages at the Burnt Oak Lane entrance to the Hollies

Foots Cray Then and Now
101. A farm cottage, Foots Cray Place
102. The pavilion in the grounds of Foots Cray Place
103-105. Foots Cray Lane
106-108. Foots Cray High Street in 1900
109. A policeman on point duty in the 1920s
110. The King's Tea Gardens, Foots Cray, *c.*1900
111. Skating on the canal in Foots Cray Place
112. A programme of entertainment, 1922
113. Birch family graves in Foots Cray churchyard
114. The Runic Cross in All Saints churchyard
115. Steam rollers in 1963
116. Footscray Meadows, 1994

Sidcup Then and Now
117 & 118. The High Street, *c.*1900
119. The crossroads by the police station, 1910
120. S. H. Wright's shop, Black Horse Road
121 & 122. Alfred Dewey's shops
123-128. The High Street
129. Woolworth's, *c.*1936
130. Robins Stores in the High Street
131. Shops in Clyde's terrace, *c.*1910
132. Hatherley Road, *c.*1905
133. Clyde Terrace and Hatherley Road, *c.*1910

134. Late Victorian houses in Hatherley Road
135 & 136. Frognal Avenue
137 & 138. The Green
139. The Manor House, 1994
140. Blackfen Public Library in Holly Park
141. Crescent Road off Station Road
142. Station Road looking towards the station
143. Station approach and Hatherley Crescent, *c.*1920s
144. Railway station and bridge, *c.*1909
145. Carlton Road
146. 'Westburton' in The Park
147 & 148. A shop in Birkbeck Road
149. Selborne Road and Rectory Lane
150. Clare Terrace at the top of Sidcup Hill in 1976
151. Sidcup Hill in 1900
152. Durham Road, *c.*1928
153. Willersley Avenue, 1968
154. Sidcup bypass in the late 1920s
155. The crossroads at Perry Street in the late 1940s
156. Main Road with Longlands Park Road in the early '20s
157. The house of Evans Nursery in Main Road
158. Old Forge Way
159. 'Maison Rouge', home of Dr. Frank Shapley
160. Memorial card for Dr. Shapley, 1899
161 & 162. Scouts and Cubs on the vicarage lawn, *c.*1928

Halfway Street, Lamorbey and Blackfen
163. Station Road in 1910
164. The corner of Hurst Road and Penhill Road
165. Church Cottages, Halfway Street
166. Lamorbey House, Halfway Street, *c.*1907
167. The *Olde Black Horse* and Lamorbey Stores
168. The Limes, Halfway Street
169. Cottages opposite the main entrance to The Hollies, *c.*1912
170. The village, Halfway Street, *c.*1910
171. Cottages opposite to Burnt Oak Lane, *c.*1900
172. The Hollies, 1994
173. No. 8 Burnt Oak Lane, 1994
174. Burnt Oak Lane, *c.*1900
175. A bridge across the Wyncham, *c.*1907
176. M. J. Sims, post office and newsagent, Halfway Street, 1957

177. Halfway Street, *c*.1920
178. Map of Montrose Park Estate in 1933
179. The Oval, soon after it was built in 1935
180. The Woodman, Blackfen, in the 1930s
181. Days Lane

North Cray
182. Almshouses in North Cray Road
183. The lodge at North Cray Place in the 1970s

Acknowledgements

I have used several books as source material. My own booklet, *The Sidcup Story* and *Foots Cray* by Gertrude Nunns are both published by Bexley Borough Libraries Service. *Discover Bexley and Sidcup* is by Darrell Spurgeon, self-published. The quotation to caption 44 comes from James Turner's book, *Seven Gardens For Catherine*. I am indebted to members of the Lamorbey and Sidcup Local History Society for furthering my knowledge of the area over many years and to the staff of the Local Studies Centre of Bexley Borough at Hall Place for all their help. I wish to thank the following for permission to take, copy or reproduce illustrations in this book: Mrs. B. Banks, 6; Mr. Roger Crane, 18; Miss S. G. Davidson, 75; Local Studies at Hall Place, 7, 14, 24, 26, 29, 30, 32, 42, 44, 47-9, 51, 53-7, 59-72, 78, 79, 81, 83, 84, 90, 92, 95, 100, 101, 103, 107, 121, 123, 126-31, 135, 148, 176, 178, 180-2; Mr. D. W. Mahoney, 97, 98, 99; my son, James Mercer, 34, 36, 50, 58, 85, 96, 105, 106, 108, 138, 177; Mr. Malcolm Youngs, 45, 46, 52, 74, 86, 87, 93, 94, 104, 119, 133, 137, 141, 142, 147, 149, 151, 156, 167, 170, 171, 174, 179; Mr. Eric Percival, 31, 43, 73, 80, 88, 89, 132, 143, 144, 152, 155, 165, 166, 169, 175; John (Doug) Sharpe, 1, 5, 12-14, 28, 112, 153; Mrs. D. Taylor, 120; Weald and Open Air Museum; 23.

The remainder are my own prints or ephemera collected over the past 30 years.

Introduction

What is Sidcup?

A major difficulty in writing a history of Sidcup is to decide where the boundaries of Sidcup lie. Sidcup began as a hamlet within the parish boundaries of Foots Cray to the north and Chislehurst to the south. Lamorbey, Halfway Street and Blackfen were regarded as part of Bexley until 1902. North Cray was always a separate parish. In 1933 the Chislehurst and Sidcup Urban District Council was established incorporating Chislehurst Urban District, Sidcup Urban District (including Foots Cray, Lamorbey, Halfway Street and Blackfen) and North Cray. In 1965 Chislehurst was placed within the London Borough of Bromley and Sidcup within the London Borough of Bexley. For the purpose of this book Sidcup will be all of the former Chislehurst and Sidcup Urban District without Chislehurst itself.

Early Development

Remains of mammals and flakes of scraper-core implements have been found in Foots Cray and North Cray, showing that prehistoric man and beast once roamed the area. Remains of a Roman settlement were found when the Bedensfield Estate, North Cray, was being laid out in 1956 by the council. Excavation uncovered a bath house and a series of buildings. It is likely that there was more than one villa on the stretch of the Cray between North Cray and Bexley. The Romano-British would have found the light gravel soils on each side of the Cray a suitable area to clear trees and to farm, utilising the water meadows for their cattle and the higher and drier land for arable farming. The river itself formed an essential means of communication. The invading Jutes took over the farmland but did not occupy the buildings, preferring to build their own wooden halls. But the first written records began with the Normans.

Place Names

Foots Cray and North Cray are both in Domesday Book. Foots Cray was named after the Saxon, Godwin Fot, presumably having an unusual foot that identified him. According to the Survey his estate was assessed at half a sulung which was an old Kentish land area used for tax assessment. There was one plough on the home farm which eight villagers shared and one and a half ploughs shared with men from a nearby estate. There were four cottagers and one serf, a mill worth 10 shillings and woods worth six pigs. The value of the estate had fallen from £4 in the reign of Edward the Confessor to £3 after the Conquest when it was held by William, son of Odger.

North Cray, like Foots Cray, takes its main name from the river Cray, a fast flowing stream that was used to power the mill mentioned above.

At the time of the Survey, in 1086, the estate was held by Ansketel of Rots and was half a sulung in area. The Lord had one plough and the seven villagers and six smallholders had one plough between them. There was one acre of meadow and three acres of pasture.

The value before 1066 when Leofric held it from King Edward was £4 and at the time of the Survey it also had dropped to £3. Halfway Street is an ancient settlement, probably taking its name from the land measurement of half a yoke and street meaning a paved way.

Lamorbey derives its name from the name of the house which was inhabited in Tudor times by the Lamienby-Sparrow family. Some 19th-century maps call the area Lamb Abbey, but there was never an abbey there.

The name Blackfen speaks for itself. Before it was built over between the two world wars it was a marshy area with many drainage channels and largely given over to strawberry growing. It was a haunt of gypsies for many generations.

Finally we come to the name of that little hamlet, Sidcup. There are two possible explanations for the name. The earliest documentary reference seems to be in 1254 when Ralph and Richard Sikecoppe appear as land owners or tenants. The two main parts of the name, 'sette' and 'copp' are respectively from the Anglo-Saxon words 'set' meaning 'fold' (as in sheep fold) and 'copp' meaning 'the top of a hill'. If one views Sidcup from Ruxley Corner it is clear that it is set on the flat top of a hill as the land rises up quite sharply from the Cray valley bottom. So whether Sidcup comes from the family name or from the land formation, a suggested evolution could be Settecopp-Sedecop-Sedcop-Sedcup-Sidcup.

Medieval Times

The local soil is not naturally productive being the infertile clays of the Woolwich and Blackheath beds with gravel and shells near the streams. Because of this there was no reason to cultivate the soil until there was a need to grow more food crops—probably about A.D. 1250. Otherwise the land would have been covered with natural vegetation, oak, elm, birch, hazel, beech, sweet chestnut (introduced by the Romans), alder, ash and willow. Smaller plants would have been blackberry, primrose and bluebell. When cultivation began, only the land that was richer or more convenient to a road was utilised; the poorer and more remote areas remained wooded. The misnamed 'The Tudors' in Foots Cray High Street, now used as offices, is, in fact, the façade of a four-bay, late mediaeval, timber-framed house. There is another well preserved medieval house in Halfway Street, also misnamed 'The Tudors', which dates from 1450. Further along Halfway Street, hidden by trees at the corner of Old Farm Avenue East, lies a second hall house, heavily altered. Until the dual carriage-way was built slicing North Cray in half there was another hall house, disguised as a general store, opposite where the 'White Cross' stands. This was dismantled and re-erected at the Open Air Museum at Singleton in West Sussex.

16th, 17th and 18th Centuries

Edward Hasted, the historian, writing in about 1775, said 'The inclosures [sic] in Kent are in general small, and consist promiscuously of arable, meadow, pasture, orchards and hop-grounds, and much woodland interspersed among them'. By that time many garden nurseries had sprung up to feed the growing populace. London was the market for most of the produce, meat 'on the hoof', vegetables, timber and charcoal. Charcoal was made in the Kemnal woods as late as 1794 and the modern *The Charcoal Burner*, on Main Road, Sidcup, is a reminder of this.

These three hundred years saw the building of several fine mansions in the district, all of which underwent improvements as new and wealthier owners took possession. The earliest, and grandest, was Frognal (probably dating from 1200), whose most famous tenants were the Sydney family (giving their name to Sydney in Australia and in Nova Scotia).

Today it lies restored but empty, waiting for use as sheltered accommodation. The site of North Cray Place is of very ancient origin. It was a manor house at the time of Henry VIII, when Sir Roger Cholmley lived there. Later the park was redesigned by 'Capability' Brown. Not far away, joined by the Five Arches bridge, was the Foots Cray Place estate. The house there was a Palladian building erected for Bourchier Cleve, a London pewterer, in 1754.

When the estate was put on the market by Bourchier Cleve's daughter, Anne, the sale catalogue for auction in the Grand Piazza of Covent Garden on 14 April 1772 described the house and grounds in flowery terms:

> That magnificent freehold villa with the park, Lawns, River Plantations and Estate ... two outbuildings, the one from a design by Inigo Jones and contains a good Brew house, a Laundry, and Washouse, with courts and menageries for breeding fowls, swine, and other conveniences ... the other stabling for 12 horses, coachouse for 4 carriages, three Harness Rooms Bed Chambers for the stablemen, Hay Lofts etc ... there is also an excellent kitchen garden in fine manurage, and in full production, walled in with cross walls, with a Hot House Green house and Ice house ... the land including the cherry orchard and canal consists of 50 acres of meadow 89 of pasture and 8 of wood on lease ... all surrounded with a pale fence in good order.

The stabling and the walled garden are still to be found there and Cleve Park School, which is built on part of the estate, is named after the original owner.

The estate passed into the Harenc family, Benjamin Harenc Senior and Benjamin Harenc Junior. The family graves are to be found in All Saints churchyard, Foots Cray, and the name has been taken by a nearby preparatory school which was formerly a Church of England Controlled School.

Lamorbey House had several owners, notably William Steele, who lived there from 1744 to 1748, and was a director of the East India Company. He and his successor, Dr. David Orme, a Scot and West Indian trader, extended it in their time. Other large houses were Sidcup Place, Sidcup House, the Manor House and Mount Mascal. Sidcup Place dates back to 1743 when the existing south-east corner was built as a square, with bastions projecting at each corner, like a 'star fort'. It is believed that it was built as the home of a retired military engineer. Today only the north-east bastion remains unaltered as the other ones have been merged into later extensions. Sidcup House was a mansion dating from the Queen Anne period, with an estate stretching back from where Market Parade now stands at the east end of the High Street to Granville Road.

The Manor House was built around 1790 for Charles Minshaw on the site of a farm. It was originally called Place Green House. Although later called the Manor House, there was never a manor of Sidcup. Mount Mascal, on the hillside to the east of North Cray, was built in the 17th century on the site of a much older house when John Mascal lived there in Tudor times. It was acquired by the Cooke family of Lesness from the Switzers. Thereafter it was owned by a succession of City of London aldermen. In its prime it was equal in size to Frognal House and larger than Foots Cray Place. The grounds were extensive including what is now known as Joydens Wood. Vale Mascal is to be found on the west side of the dual carriageway and backs on to the River Cray, built in 1746. It is a more modest residence having been considerably altered in recent years.

Most of the houses mentioned above were built by so-called 'Nabobs', men who had made their money in India or by trading in the West Indies. They wanted their country houses to be within easy reach of London as many had second homes there. As much of the land was wooded and relatively unproductive it was cheap to buy. There were also layers of clay suitable for brick manufacture. In the next century north-west Kent was to supply much of London's requirements for the familiar yellow stock bricks.

Roads and Coaching Inns of the 18th Century

The road through Foots Cray was a major highway. It was the road from London to Maidstone and on to the Kentish ports. There were no less than five inns in Foots Cray, of which the *Tiger's Head* provided for stage coaches. Burnt down in 1792 it was quickly rebuilt, and in a sale catalogue of 1820 it advertised stabling for 50 horses, and 16 stage coaches each day. It stood where Robert Greig's supermarket is situated.

In Sidcup the *Black Horse* dates from 1705. In 1775, Hasted wrote that Sidcup was, 'a small street of houses, among which is an inn of much resort'. In 1786, the inn was a post stage on the London-Hythe road and horses could be changed there. In 1781, Sidcup Hill was turnpiked by the New Cross Turnpike Trust. Before then the route to Foots Cray went down Rectory Lane. There is still a turnpike cottage near Ruxley Corner and one of the tollbooths used to be in Sidcup High Street near where Woolworth's is now situated. The road from Chislehurst followed across The Green (Elm Road was built in the last century) passing, as it still does, the old farm building, now called Place Cottage. Station Road was built when the railway came in 1865, but the narrow lanes leading to Bexley had been carved out as field boundaries for many centuries, i.e. Bexley Lane, Foots Cray Lane, Hurst Road (once called Bexley Lane, too) and Burnt Oak Lane. Halfway Street linked Bexley with Eltham and possessed a second *Black Horse*. It is not known if this one is older than the one in the High Street. Probably the oldest pub of all is the *Seven Stars* in Foots Cray, dating at least from the 15th century. Its gardens back on to where the old mill used to be. In wet weather Foots Cray High Street must have been a sea of mud and horse manure and during a hot summer the smell must have been pungent! We complain today of petrol fumes and air pollution but forget the odours of the past which were particularly bad in built-up places.

The 19th century

In the first three quarters of the 19th century the district was dominated by several important and wealthy families. The Townshends in Frognal (the Lords Sydney) were aristocrats of several generations. The third Viscount, John Robert Townshend, was Lord Chamberlain to Queen Victoria and, after her visit to Frognal in 1872, he was elevated to an earldom. Dame Ethel Smythe, the composer, who lived in Sidcup House when a child, described him as '... the most pompous old gentleman I have ever seen, with his curled grey whiskers and gold pince-nez ... Lady Sydney was rather a dear, I used to think.'

Nicholas Vansittart, 1st Baron Bexley, acquired Foots Cray Place and North Cray Place in 1822 when he ceased to be Chancellor of the Exchequer and took his seat in the House of Lords. He was a keen evangelical churchman, bitterly opposed to the emancipation of the Roman Catholics in 1829 by his colleague the Duke of Wellington. He was a supporter of the Bible Society and put up some of the money for the building of the first church of St John the Evangelist in Sidcup. He was also a patron of the local National School (now Harenc School) and delighted in having all the children to summer tea on the lawns of his estate. He died in 1851, leaving a nephew as heir. In 1872, Sir John Pender, the entrepreneur responsible for the laying of a vast network of submarine cables, became the tenant until his death in 1898. There is a dramatic Runic Cross in All Saints churchyard which marks the resting place of him and his family.

Lord Castlereagh, the Foreign Secretary during the second Napoleonic War, acquired North Cray Cottage as a country residence adjacent to London. He committed suicide there in 1822, by cutting his throat with a razor. The cottage, now called Loring Hall, dates from 1760 and is in reality a fine stuccoed mansion, used today as a nursing home.

The Malcolms inherited the Lamorbey Estate from Dr. Orme, whose daughter married John Malcolm. The Malcolm family lived there from 1812 until the 1870s, but retained ownership until 1910. They carried out many alterations, rebuilding in Jacobean style the east and south fronts. The most interesting rooms are the library, the music room and the art room which date from the 1840s. Mary Malcolm, one of the first television announcers, is a grandchild of the family.

The Hollies was an estate owned by the Lewins. Like so many of the gentry in the district, they made their wealth with the East India Company. The present house was built *c.*1853 on the site of a much older house called Marrowbone Hall. At the turn of the century the estate was sold for development and in 1901 the Greenwich and Deptford Board of Guardians set up a self-contained village for over 500 children, retaining the big house as its administrative centre. The architect was Thomas Dinwiddy (1845-1926), and the concept of cottages for the children taken into care supervised by a house mother or father became the pattern for other institutions at home and abroad.

The Berens lived in Sidcup Place from 1822 until 1919. They were city magnates who extended the original core building in 1853 and again in 1896. There is a long ha-ha of knapped flint and extensive views across the Cray valley to Joydens Wood and beyond. Henry Berens put up most of the money for the church of St John the Evangelist, and also built Ursula Lodges on Sidcup Hill for retired governesses who had to be single and of the Established Church. There were six lodges each with accommodation for a servant and two school rooms above in which the governesses could teach Sunday School children, one room for each sex. These were completed in 1847 (replaced by sheltered accommodation in 1972). A snapshot of Sidcup at the time of the Reform Bill of 1832 would show great social differences: aristocratic landowners, gentry (from the lesser land-owning classes or the learned professions), merchants in trade (rising into the gentry often by marriage), artisans and shopkeepers, agricultural labourers and the indigent poor.

By the end of the 19th century there are still great social differences but the social pattern has changed. Gone or going are the aristocrats. The mansions are occupied by gentry often achieving fame and fortune by trade or industry. The ranks of the middle classes have expanded enormously. Sidcup has become a dormitory for architects, bankers, accountants, doctors, lawyers and actuaries who have offices or chambers in the city or Westminster. The artisans have expanded too, as the rising population required skilled builders, plumbers, house decorators and clerks. The shopkeepers and their assistants have increased in number as have the domestic servants. The agricultural labourers have declined in number as the fields and woods have been progressively built on. The chief agent of change has been the coming of the railway.

The Coming of the Railway

The railway from Charing Cross to Dartford was opened in 1865. It had a dramatic effect upon the neighbourhood. The greatest effect was in housing. Station Road was built with large detached and semi-detached houses for the professional classes who could travel to London by train. Hatherley Road soon followed and thereafter Carlton Road and the Park. James Turner, who lived in the Park, wrote of his father:

'No one who saw my father setting out for his London office in a frock coat, or one of our neighbours, the dapper Mr. Barham, an accountant, in his top hat and with a carnation in his buttonhole could ever refer to such men as commuters. They were Professional men, a grade below the gentry who lived in Chislehurst.'

For the artisans, Birkbeck Road and its adjoining roads developed smaller editions of the middle-class houses. Many display the date of construction—1870, 1875, 1880. The High Street was filled with shops, grocers, greengrocers, butchers, hardware, haberdasheries—and all would deliver to their customers. Behind modern shop-fronts are the original buildings of the 1870s. A major builder was George Hawkins, whose trade mark was semi-Norman dog-tooth arches. There are a number of these houses surviving. Later, Thomas Knight built the neat estate off Sidcup Hill—Oxford Road, Lincoln Road, Sussex Road and Warwick Road—in the pre-1914 years. Similar small properties were built along and off Main Road, while more substantial houses were built in Stafford Road and Northcote Road, but none so grand as those built in the Crescent and Christchurch Road. Foots Cray during this time sank into poverty; there was little if any building activity there as Sidcup expanded and replaced Foots Cray as the main residential area. North Cray remained a farming area, while Halfway Street and Blackfen continued to be rural village and low-lying open land, respectively.

With this expansion, there was a corresponding growth in churches and schools. The old parishes had had their churches for centuries. St James, North Cray, may well be the oldest on site, possibly dating from 1120. It was almost entirely rebuilt in 1852, in ragstone with a steeple and shingled spire. Much of the interior woodwork dates from the 15th century. All Saints, Foots Cray, is basically 13th-century but it was rebuilt by Henry Hakewell around 1863. The tower is made of wood and is over the central part of the nave. The medieval remains within comprise a very wide arch to the chantry chapel, a Norman font and a monument to Lady de Vaughan. The next oldest church is Foots Cray Baptist, in Sidcup Hill, built in 1836. It has a churchyard in front of its Gothic façade of 1885, with a large tomb in memory of John Rogers, grocer and Sunday School teacher, who died from burns caused by a spilled lamp when ministering in the chapel room. It was the same John Rogers who carried out the 1851 Census return for the village. The church of St John the Evangelist, Sidcup, was first built in 1844 (see the earlier entry about its promoters), enlarged in 1882 and rebuilt yet again to house a congregation of 1,000 in 1900. This expansion demonstrates the phenomenal growth of Sidcup from 1865 onwards. Holy Trinity, Lamorbey, began as a chapel-of-ease in 1840, and was rebuilt as a Gothic church in 1879 by Ewan Christian (1814-1895). The Malcolms were the patrons of both enterprises. The oldest school was the National School in Foots Cray, built in 1815. It was patronised by the Harencs and Lord Bexley. In its opening years the children attended from 9 a.m. until 12 a.m. and from 2 p.m. until 5 p.m. (or dusk in winter), with half holidays on Wednesday and Saturday, but attendance twice on Sunday. Each child paid one penny a week towards the school fund from which rewards for merit and punctuality were given out. The children were expected to '... come with their faces, ears and hands clean, their hair cut short and well combed or washed and their clothes well mended at least on Sunday'.

In 1883 the school was rebuilt. The marks made by pupils sharpening their slate pencils can still be seen on the wall by the entrance to the school.

Mrs. Malcolm of Lamorbey House opened a school in 1841 which became a National School on a new site in Hurst Road in 1880. Both buildings survive, the first as a private cottage at the beginning of Burnt Oak Lane and the second as the parish hall of Holy Trinity Church. North Cray National School opened in North Cray Road in 1860. It is now converted into two private houses. Birkbeck National School was built in Birkbeck Road, on land given by Charlotte Berens of Sidcup Place. It came under the aegis of St John's. It is noteworthy that up to the end of the century all elementary schools in the district were under the control of the Church of England. There were also several private schools, catering for the middle classes, that flourished and then declined.

The Country Houses

Frognal went under the hammer and became the nursing quarters in the First World War for the Queen's Hospital. Foots Cray Place became the residence of Lord Waring, the director of Waring and Gillows. After the Second World War it was acquired by the Kent Education Committee to become a schools museum, but was burnt down by a tramp in 1949. Lamorbey House became a hotel in 1910, but after the Second World War it, too, was acquired by the K.C.C. and turned into an Adult Education Centre. It is now leased by Bexley Borough to the Rose Bruford College of Speech and Drama but still has accommodation for adult students. Mount Mascal remained empty for some years, then was used for war-time emergency housing. In 1957 it was demolished and flats were built on the site. The Hollies was put on sale for prime development in 1982 and many of the former children's cottages and institution buildings have been converted; the estate has been made a conservation area. Sidcup House was pulled down in 1929 and replaced by shops and housing. Sidcup Place was briefly a boys' school, before it became the offices of the Chislehurst and Sidcup Urban District Council in 1934. It now houses the Directorate of Engineering and Works of the London Borough of Bexley. The Manor House is also in local authority hands. It has recently been refurbished as a Registry Office and also houses the Social Services Department.

The First World War

The Queen's Hospital was established in the grounds of Frognal in 1917 for the treatment of sailors and soldiers with facial and jaw injuries. A collection of pre-fabricated huts was assembled to which injured men were brought by boat and train from the battlefront. It became internationally famous for the advances made in facial plastic surgery by Major Harold Gillies (later Sir Harold). The hospital was temporary, designed to last for 10 years, but as Queen Mary's from 1930 it utilised the old huts until a new series of buildings was completed in 1974, opened by Barbara Castle, the then Secretary of State.

New Housing

The slump in farming, that so damaged agriculture after the First World War, made farm-land very cheap and speculative builders moved into the area north of the railway, hitherto relatively untouched by housing development. Days Farm and Vinsons Farm and areas formerly owned by the Lewins of the Hollies were sold off to the New Ideal Home Estates and other developers. Houses were mass produced (the first time that pre-fabricated homes were manufactured). The new housing might have been cheap, but it was not 'jerry-built' as the condition of these properties today testifies. The New Ideal Homes, which built much of this stock, used pre-fabricated materials. Bricks came from Belgium and windows from Czechoslovakia, and were brought ashore at Erith only four miles away. With a low-paid work force on piece rates, encouraged to work overtime, a house could be built in three weeks. Soon Blackfen and Hurst Road and Penhill were covered with small but cheap houses to buy, offering the latest in comfort and convenience. The Oval was designed to be a superior shopping centre for the upper working-class immigrants from South-East London. Houses were to buy, not rent, but, with low interest rates and cheap mortgages, the new estates proved highly attractive. The private housing boom of the 1930s helped to lift Britain out of the Great Depression.

The Second World War

During the 'Blitz' of 1940-1 there was indiscriminate bombing all over London by night and tip-and-run raiding by day. Most enemy aircraft headed for the greater density of London, but Sidcup had its fair share of bombs and casualties. A noteworthy casualty was Doug Holland's forge in Cross Road at the top of Sidcup Hill. 'Queen Mary's' was bombed in 1941. Three wards were hit and 17 patients and three staff members were killed. But the worst time was endured during the attack by V1s and V2s in 1944-5. It was then that the suburbs received the greater damage. The heaviest incident was in March 1945, when a V2 rocket fell on to Shepherd's Garage at the top of Sidcup Hill and caused nine deaths and 53 casualties. A rocket destroyed the Odeon Cinema (now Lamorbey Baths) and much of Holy Trinity Church across the road.

Since the Second World War

The 1944 Education Act led to several new secondary schools being established to augment the local authority schools built earlier in the century. Chislehurst and Sidcup Grammar School was rebuilt in Hurst Road on land previously used by Sidcup Golf Club. Hurstmere was built close by as a secondary modern school, taking the boys from Blackfen School which became exclusively for girls. Cleve Park took boys and girls from the old Central School buildings in Alma Road to become co-educational. The former Girls' County School in Station Road became the Bexley Music Centre. A fine new Holy Trinity School by Oliver Steer was built in Burnt Oak Lane in 1969 to become the only church school left in the area. Two old established private schools are West Lodge in Station Road and Merton Court in Knoll Road.

Since the turn of the century there has been further church building. Christ Church in Main Road, Sidcup, developed as a break away church from St John's, which became too 'high' for some of the parishioners. The Roman Catholic St Lawrence of Canterbury was built in 1906 and has a large and handsome classical house of 1924 which became a home for the Marist Fathers. Holy Redeemer in Days Lane, the Church of the Good Shepherd, and Days Lane Baptist Church are modern buildings reflecting the perceived need for new places of worship among the post 1914-18 war housing developments.

In 'Old Sidcup' there has been heavy destruction of the larger properties. Flats and maisonettes have replaced older and more handsome houses. There has been in-filling between houses with gardens considered too large by their owners. At first, planning permission was easily obtained and some poorly-designed and badly-built properties were constructed. More recently the planning authorities have measured up to their responsibilities and in-filling and property development is much more strictly controlled. Sidcup has been zoned as residential and for office development. Foots Cray is the area for industrial growth. Green Belt status has been designated to grounds formerly belonging to Foots Cray Place and land east of North Cray Road, while land around Frognal and in other green areas is protected as Metropolitan Open Space. Forty-one per cent of all office space within the London Borough of Bexley is located in Sidcup and includes Marlowe House, a tall block by the railway station.

Old amongst the New

An account has already been given of the surviving great houses and their estates. There are some less obvious historic properties that have also survived. Rectory Lane, Foots Cray, has four imposing early Georgian red-brick houses in a terrace known as Belgrave Place, by the crossroads. It has a brick inscribed 1737, but it is believed that the terrace was built around 1760. At one time the block was known as the work-house cottages, but there is no evidence that it was ever thus used. Next to it lies 'The Old House', dating from 1820, although it is thought that there is some Tudor work within. Not far away, at the bottom of Sidcup Hill, is Walnut Tree Cottage, *c*.1550. It is a timber-framed house, refaced in the 1930s but with a modern porch. In North Cray, next to the former National School, are two cottages; Pear Tree Cottage dates from 1790, and Rose Cottage (once two) is much earlier, *c*.1600, and timber-framed. Halfway Street contains a remarkable group of old houses, which formed the nucleus of the old hamlet of Halfway Street. There is the White House (*c*.1877), Lilac Cottage (*c*.1800), Tudor Cottage (1450), Halfway Cottage (*c*.1830), Fern Cottage (*c*.1840), Farm Cottage (*c*.1500) and Old Farm (late 19th-century extension). At the foot of Hatherley Road lie 'The Old Ladies', a group of tall houses, *c*.1870. They were built with a profusion of ornamentation: chevron and dogtooth decorations and stonework with detailing of birds, animals, fruit and leaves. A modern development which is quite outstanding is Old Forge Way, off Rectory Lane, Sidcup. The houses are of 17th- and 18th-century style of the Weald, designed by Kenneth Dalgleish in 1936. The upper floors are tile-hung, weatherboarded or half-timbered, and the ground floors of red brick.

Despite the 20th-century development of small houses and street after street covering what was once farm or woodland, Sidcup preserves a rural element because of the preserved estates, parks and small woodland. Moreover there are many tree-lined avenues especially in the Lamorbey and Blackfen area, while to the east the sweep of Foots Cray Meadows and the open land east of North Cray make one aware that the Kent countryside is close. Sidcup is very much on the edge of London and although 'Old Sidcup' has been swamped, it is not difficult to imagine the stately days when Viscount Sydney, Lord Bexley, the Berens, the Lewins and the Malcolms rode across their lands and enjoyed the shooting rights across the farms.

Sources

The Sidcup Story, John Mercer (Bexley Library and Museums Department) 1988. Reprint 1992.

Foots Cray, Gertrude Nunns (Bexley Library and Museums Department) 1982.

Discover Bexley and Sidcup, Darrell Spurgeon (Greenwich Guide Books) 1993.

Old Maps

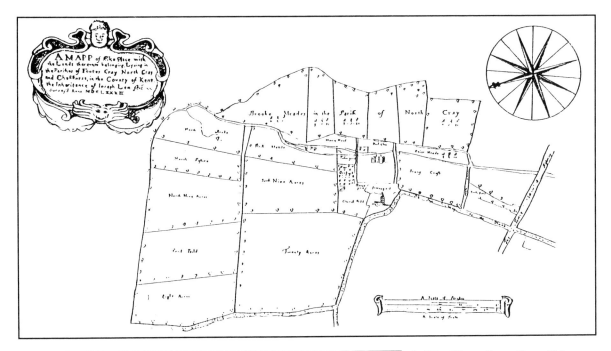

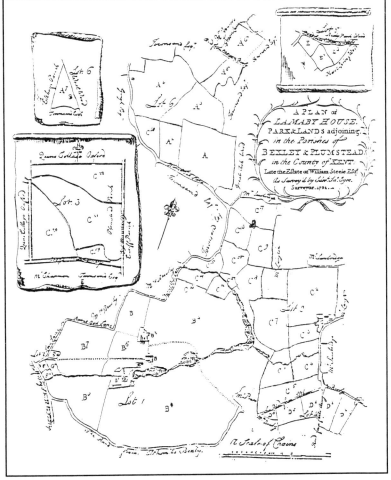

1. Pike Place, Foots Cray, This manor house was behind All Saints church and in the possession of Joseph Lem in 1683. It fell into ruin and was demolished when Foots Cray Place was built.

2. Estate map of Lamorbey House upon the sale in 1761 occasioned by the death of William Steele Esq. The house is marked B and the coach house B2.

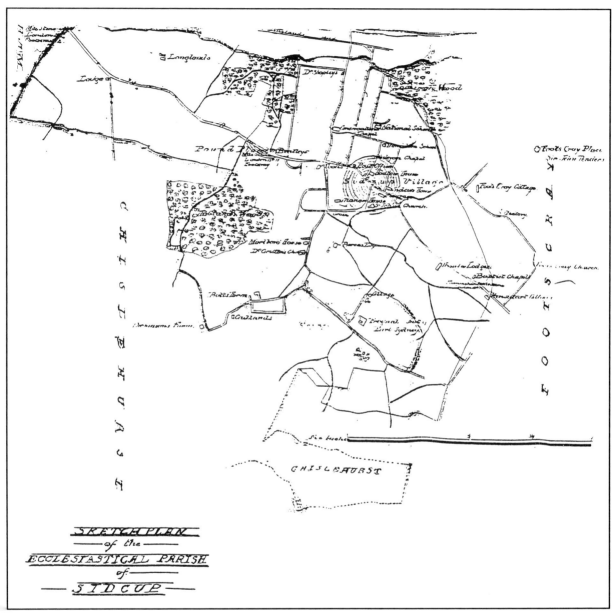

3. Map of the parish of St John the Evangelist, *c.*1886, during the incumbency of the Rev. T. C. Lewis. Note the circling of what was considered to be Sidcup village. To many elderly residents it was still called 'the village' until quite recently.

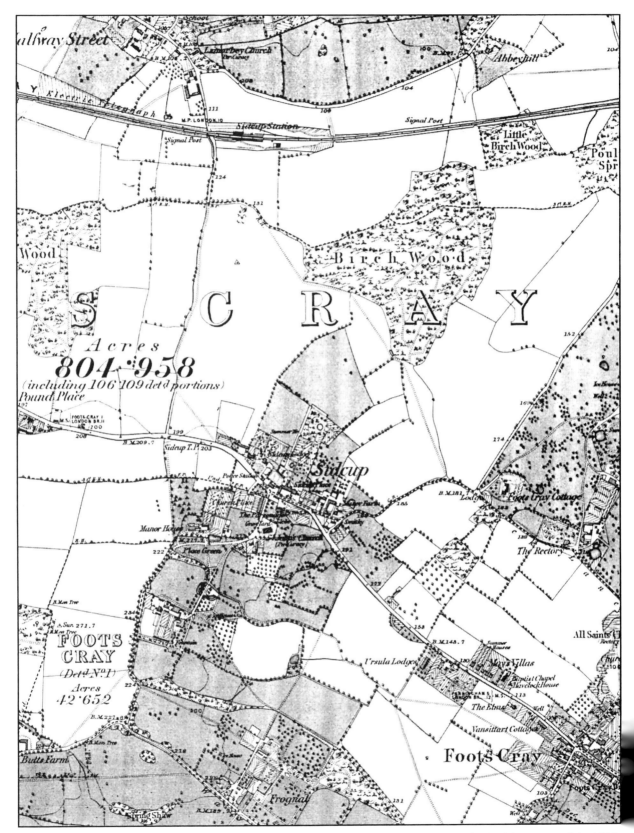

4. OS 25" Map of Sidcup in 1869 showing Foots Cray and Halfway Street. The railway line had been opened in 1866. Note that Foots Cray was still considered to be the more important area.

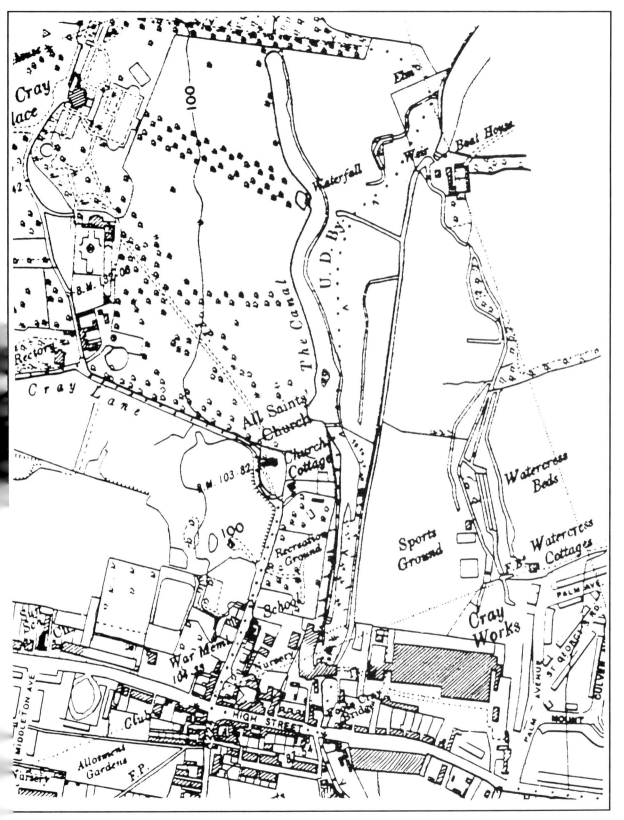

5. An enlargement of an OS map of the 1930s showing Foot Cray village. Note Church Cottage, the canal with the waterfall at the end of the line of lime trees, the boat house on the east side of the Cray, and the watercress beds with Watercress Cottage.

Stately Homes and Old Houses

6. Frognal House, the seat of Viscount Sydney. The oldest mansion in Sidcup dating from at least 1200, re-built in 1670 and again in the 18th century. Queen Victoria came here in 1872 to award Lord Sydney an earldom (he was her Lord Chamberlain). W. E. Gladstone admired the great oak tree, and Conan Doyle set one of his Sherlock Holmes stories in the house.

7. Frognal House, when it became medical quarters in 1917 and was renamed Queen's Hospital.

8. North Cray Place. The manor of North Cray is mentioned in Domesday Book. In the reign of Richard I it belonged to a family called Rokesle, whose name survives in the nearby 'lost' hamlet of Ruxley. In 1778 the manor was inherited by Thomas Coventry who engaged the services of 'Capability' Brown to re-design the park around the house. This print by Bayly from the first edition of Hasted's *History of Kent* shows the garden and grounds as they were shortly before Brown altered them in 1782. It was completely rebuilt by Coventry in 1822-3 and pulled down in 1962, having suffered from major bomb damage in 1944.

9. North Cray Cottage was built *c*.1760 and was the country house of Lord Castlereagh, the Foreign Secretary in Lord Liverpool's administration during the second war (1803-1815) with Napoleon Bonaparte. He is remembered for the boundary settlement between the United States and Canada, the 49th Parallel. He is also remembered for his suicide in the cottage in 1822, due to stress of work and a hostile press. The building is now Loring Hall, a nursing home.

10. Foots Cray Place. This was built in the Palladian style in 1754 by Isaac Ware for Bourchier Cleve, a London pewterer. Later it was the home of Benjamin Harenc, another London merchant. Nicholas Vansittart, Chancellor of the Exchequer under Liverpool, acquired the property when he was ennobled as Lord Bexley in 1822. Lord Bexley later acquired North Cray Place. He died in 1851. The two most notable residents were Sir John Pender, the pioneer of submarine telegraphy, and Lord Waring of Waring and Gillows. During the Second World War it was occupied by the training ship *Worcester*. In 1949 a fire, which was accidentally started, destroyed the building and it had to be demolished. Had the fire not occurred it would have become a museum under the Kent Education Authority.

11. A postcard sent in 1926 shows Foots Cray Place from the terrace. Lord Waring was then in residence.

12. A youth section of the Camping Club of Great Britain and Ireland, taken on the edge of Foots Cray Place terrace in 1949. 'Jock' Gurr is on the right. Shortly after the picture was taken the mansion was burnt down.

13. Sidcup Girl Crusaders on the front step of Foots Cray Place. The photograph was taken in 1938 or 1939.

14. The Five Arches Bridge over the Cray. This was probably built at the time of the 1782 reconstruction of the North Cray Estate by 'Capability' Brown but could have been an addition by Lord Bexley when he owned the two estates.

15. Vale Mascal, a charming 18th-century residence backing on to the River Cray and still used as a private family house by Mr. and Mrs. R. Grant.

16.   Lamorbey House was re-built from a medieval manor house in 1744 and 1784. The first owner was Thomas Sparrow, the deputy reeve of the manor of Bexley in 1455. It passed to his daughter Agnes who married a Goldwell. They built a new house and called it Lamienby-Goldwell—hence the modern name. The Malcolms lived there from the end of the 18th century until the mid-19th century. It was a hotel from 1910 until 1946 when it became an adult education centre. It is now leased from the borough by the Rose Bruford College.

17. The lake at Lamorbey House.

18. The coach house of Lamorbey House. When Lamorbey House was a hotel the coach house housed 13 members of staff and included 22 public bedrooms. The hotel was owned by Mr. H. J. Sheppard from 1923 until 1945.

19. Sidcup Place, Chislehurst Road, was built in 1743 and added to substantially in 1852 and 1886 by the Berens family. It became Sidcup Hall College in 1907 and after the First World War it became a preparatory school under Rev. J. W. Blencowe, former army chaplain to the neighbouring Queen's Hospital. In 1934 the newly-formed Chislehurst and Sidcup Urban District Council acquired the property for their offices and the grounds were opened to the public.

20. The oldest occupied dwelling in the area. It is known as 'Tudor Cottage' but is much older than the name suggests, having been a yeoman's house from 1452. It is in Halfway Street where several other old properties can be found.

21. The Hollies was built around 1852 for the Lewins who had made their money in the City and in the East India Company. A former house called 'Marrowbone Hall' lay somewhere to the west of the present building. This photograph was taken in 1986 when the house was empty following the closure of the Children's Home, originally developed by the Greenwich and Deptford Board of Guardians. It housed the administration offices.

22. The medieval North Cray Hall House was built in the 15th century. When the North Cray Road was widened in the late 1960s the village general store was demolished. It turned out to be a medieval hall with smoke blackened beams—caused by the smoke from the fires lit in the hall escaping through a hole in the roof. The late Mr. Peter Tester discovered its ancient origins and in due course the hall was taken down piece by piece and re-built in the Open Air Museum at Singleton, Sussex.

23. The building on the right is the North Cray Hall House as reconstructed in the Weald and Downland Museum, Singleton. It has had the elm beams painted red as was discovered when the timbers were taken down.

24. The Old House, Church Road, Foots Cray. This is believed to have Tudor origins and in its present form dates from 1818.

25. The terrace of Queen Anne three-storey houses next door to the 'Old House', known as Belgrave Place. These date from about 1737 and tradition has it that French prisoners of war were once housed here. They were also known as 'The Workhouse Cottages' but there is no evidence that they were ever used in that capacity.

26. Tudor Cottages seen on the right of this illustration of Foots Cray High Street, *c*.1923. Once again they are not Tudor but date from the middle of the 15th century. The original property was a four-bay timber-framed house. Happily the façade has been preserved. Only these cottages, now offices, and the *Red Lion* are left of the old High Street.

27. Walnut Tree Cottage is believed to date from 1664 although it has been considerably altered. At one time it was the home of the coachman to 'The Elms' which stood on the site of the present Sidcup Hill Gardens. Before that a tollgate made by James Mandy (a local carpenter) was built near to the cottage in 1808 for the New Cross Turnpike Trust, which had made a new road, Sidcup Hill, in 1781.

28. Church Cottage, Church Road, Foots Cray. It is reputed that the painter, J. M. W. Turner (1775-1851), stayed here in his youth. The last occupier was a Mrs. Butcher. The cottage was demolished in the 1950s.

Churches and Chapels

29. St James', North Cray. The earliest reference to a church at North Cray dates from 1120. The present church is of ragstone, rebuilt by Edwin Nash in 1852 and shown here. The churchyard is largely surrounded by the 18th-century kitchen garden walls of the former North Cray Place. To the west of the church is an impressive iron gate which led to the big house itself and to Five Arches Bridge.

30. A more recent photograph of the church taken from Foots Cray Meadows, *c*.1920s. North Cray Place lies to the right.

31. All Saints, Foots Cray, a postcard view sent to a Mrs. Garwood of Linstead Parva in Suffolk in 1909. The writer must have been a maid and wrote on the card, 'My mistress is going under the operation on Wednesday. I have been so busy'. Is this the carriage of the Rector, the Rev. Charles Birch? We know that he had a coachman.

32. All Saints, Foots Cray, a photograph taken about the same time as the postcard. The trees show a different season and the cemetery has been added to, but otherwise much is identical.

33. St John the Evangelist. This was the original church built in 1844 and dedicated by George Murray, Bishop of Rochester on 16 April of that year. It was built as a district church in the parish of Chislehurst largely by contributions from Lord Sydney, Lord Bexley and Harold Berens Esq. The first minister was the Rev. Samuel Holmes who was priest-in-charge.

34. As Sidcup grew the Rev. T. C. Lewis built a new chancel (largely at his own expense) and then an addition was made to the nave. This photograph shows the church from the north-west as it was between 1882 and 1898. The next incumbent described this second church building as the ugliest in Kent, and likened the extension to a shooting gallery.

35. The Rev. T. C. Lewis was responsible for the building of the National School in Birkbeck Road, for which the land was given in memory of Charlotte Berens of Sidcup Place. His incumbency (1882-86) was brought to a tragic end. Whilst playing in the vicarage garden, his six-year-old son accidentally shot his mother with a rook gun and the wound proved to be fatal. Mr. Lewis returned to his native Devonshire and became vicar of Dodsworth until he died in 1912.

36. The third and present St John's was built between 1899 and 1901. The architect was Fellowes Prynne. It was built to hold a thousand people as expanding Sidcup needed an even larger church. All that remains of the 1844 building are part of the flint and brick outer wall, and the chancel built in 1882.

37. St John's church as seen from the Green in 1910. The tree is no longer there, nor the seat.

38. The Rev. C. E. Shirley Woolmer who followed the Rev. Lewis and inspired the building of the third church. He disliked the custom of eating hot cross buns on Good Friday and would give the choir boys sixpence each to stop them. He died suddenly in 1902 leaving his successor, the Rev. E. B. Spurgin, an enormous debt to clear.

39. The chancel and altar of St John the Evangelist before the memorial screen was erected to the memory of Shirley Woolmer.

40. The nave of St John's showing the elaborate screen put up shortly after the death of Rev. Shirley Woolmer in 1902.

41. A procession leaving Hatherley Road on its way to St John's from Birkbeck School, *c*.1907, probably to commemorate Ascension Day.

42. Holy Trinity, Lamorbey. This was funded by the Malcolms of Lamorbey House and is a Victorian Gothic ragstone building designed by Ewan Christian in 1879. It was badly damaged by a V2 rocket in 1945 and rebuilt in replication. The original vicarage is Abbeyhill, in Hurst Road.

43. The nave and chancel of Holy Trinity was built in 1879 to resemble a medieval interior. Here it can be seen shortly after it was completed.

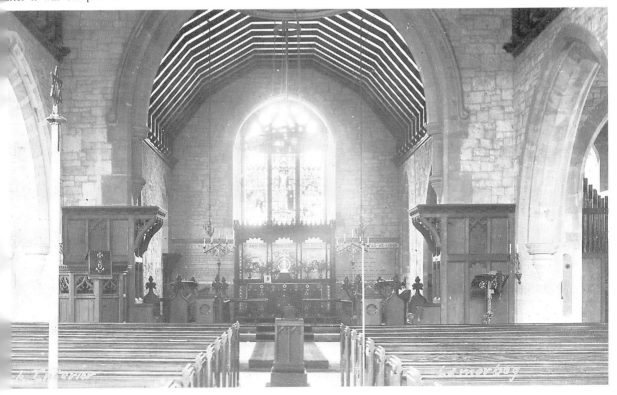

44. The Iron church in Chislehurst Road, near where Upperton Road is now. When the Rev. R. H. M. Berens was vicar of St John's he introduced vestments, candles and a robed choir in accordance with his Tractarian beliefs. This offended many in the congregation who left and set up their own church in 1878. They built the iron church and worshipped there until they could have their own parish. As a result the parish of Christ church was established and a new stone built church was consecrated in 1901. Among the original dissenters from High Church practices were Lord Sydney of Frognal and Charles Edward O'Shea of The Elms, Foots Cray.

45. Christ Church in Main Road is a large ragstone building. There is a corrugated iron shed at the south east which hides the place where preparations were made to build a tower. The interior is lofty with a high chancel arch.

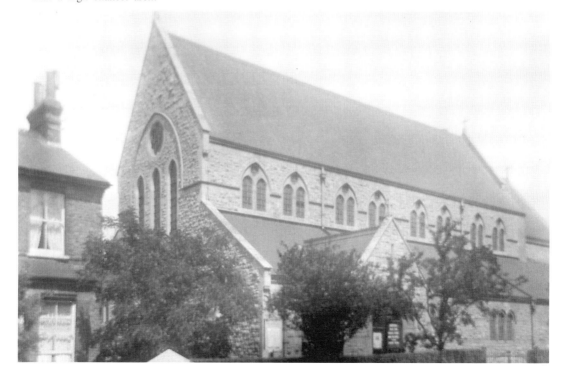

46. The Congregational church in Station Road was built in 1888 by George Baines. It is now the Sidcup Community church and the interior has been modernised.

47. The Methodist church (formerly known as the Wesleyan) at the corner of Hadlow Road and Granville Road. According to Walsham's *Sidcup Directory* of 1894, 'The present School Chapel being inadequate to the requirements of the congregation, arrangements are being made to erect a larger building as soon as the necessary funds can be raised'. The minister then was the Rev. E. M. Jackson. It is now the Emmanuel church combining the Methodist and United Reform churches.

48. Sidcup Baptist chapel in Hatherley Road next to the Public Hall. The photograph was taken in the early 1920s. Beckets Honda Garage is to be found there now, while the chapel has moved to Main Road.

The Railway

49 & 50. A steam-hauled passenger train (*right*) pulling into Sidcup station in the 1890s and (*below*) the station, *c*.1900. Between 1871 and 1911 Sidcup's population increased from 390 to 8,493 reflecting the dramatic impetus to development following the construction of the railway. There were three classes of rail travel: first, second and third. Third class was abandoned in the 1930s.

51. A coal delivery from C. J. Cockerell & Co. at Sidcup station approach in the 1920s.

52. A different kind of railway! According to the postcard this was in Sidcup Place, but the author thinks it more likely to have been in Waring Park some time in the 1930s.

The Fire Service

53. The Sidcup Fire Brigade on parade and proudly displaying their trophies. F.C.U.D.C. on the plaque above the door relates to the time prior to 1921 when the building was the offices of the Foots Cray Urban District Council. This photograph and the following must have been taken shortly afterwards.

54. One of the fire tenders seen in the preceding picture but this time carrying men and not ladders.

55. The rear of the fire station in Main Road. An off duty fireman and a gardener pose for the camera. Today this area is fully concreted over and has a tower for drying the hoses.

Farming and Country Pursuits

56. Hop picking in Halfway Street before the First World War. Once the hops had been picked it was taken to be dried at one of several oast houses that used to be in Halfway Street.

57. Hop pickers and a gunner, possibly home on leave, pose for the camera in 1915. Most of the hops collected went to Reffell's Brewery which was situated in nearby Bexley village.

58. Hop pickers on Vinson's Farm, Days Lane, during the First World War. Those pictured are members of the Jenner and Ellis families from nearby Bexleyheath.

59. Holly Park Farmhouse, Halfway Street. It stood on the north side of Halfway Street alongside the stream by Wyncham Bridge. It was built in 1888 and demolished in 1932. The farm grew 60 acres of vegetables for the London market. In front are Mrs. Helen Barker, on the left, and Mrs. Hayes, her mother, on the right. At the side is Mrs. Ada Hawkins, her friend. The photograph was taken before 1912. The Barker family farmed it until its demolition.

60. All the family stop to have their photograph taken in the hop fields at Longmeadow Road.

61. Hay making in the 1920s.

62. Mr. F. A. Johnson of Foots Cray picking watercress from the extensive beds in 1938. The presence of the watercress beds led to several outbreaks of typhoid in the 19th century, including the children at the Foots Cray National School and in 1899 the untimely death, at the age of 42, of Dr. Frank Shapley, the Medical Officer of Health.

63. La Retraite Nursery in Blackfen with 1930s housing going up around it, looking towards houses in Ronaldstone Road. *The Jolly Fenman* now stands on the site.

64. The old Golf Club Pavilion off Church Avenue, now the Sidcup Social and Recreation Club. The golf course used to be where the allotments and Cray Wanderers Football Ground now is.

65. Sheep on the old golf links in October 1905. Sheep and cattle were often brought to graze on this land which is now held by Queen Mary's hospital and Sidcup Place.

66. The new Golf House off Hurst Road and adjacent to Lamorbey House, taken in 1915.

67. The oast houses at Hurst Farm in 1949 prior to demolition. The farm stood next to Hurst Place Community Centre where Stanstead Crescent is now.

68. Raspberry picking in the Blackfen area in the early 1930s. Note the cloche hats.

69. The Lait family on their doorstep at 4 Glen Cottages, Blackfen, in the early 1920s.

70. Doug Holland's forge at Cross Road. This was where Sidcup grew as a hamlet before becoming a village. Doug Holland was an ex-army farrier and took over the forge in 1925 when he left the army. The forge was bombed in 1940 but re-opened quickly and was in regular use until the 1960s.

71. Smokey Joe was a well-known character around the district between the 1920s and 1960s. He lived rough, begged, was often given food on a regular basis and was taken in by the police to be looked after from time to time. He caused no harm but sometimes frightened the nervous. He died in hospital.

72. The Old Folks at Home. The situation and the couple are unknown, but they are in 19th-century dress. Could it be the thatched cottage in Perry Street, now in Chislehurst?

Hospitals

73. Queen's Hospital in 1917. Frognal House had become the administrative centre and nursing quarters after being sold before the outbreak of the First World War.

74. The Queen's Hospital was established for the treatment of servicemen with facial and jaw injuries. Major Harold Gillies (later Sir Harold) became internationally famous for his work in plastic surgery. Here are some of the patients. They wore blue coats, white shirts and red ties when walking out and became familiar figures in the town. The wounded arrived by train at Sidcup station and were ferried up to the hospital by bus and horsedrawn vehicles.

75. Christmas Day 1917 in Ward 6 at Queen's Hospital.

76. Queen's Hospital Football Team. Patients whose features had been restored.

77. The visit of Her Majesty The Queen on 13 November 1917. Major Gillies is standing on the right and the Matron (second from the right) was Miss Barber. A ward in the new Queen Mary's is named after Dr. Gillies and a block of the nurses' accommodation is named after Miss Barber.

78. Some of the hutted wards. These were in use in Queen Mary's Hospital until 1974 when the new hospital was opened by Barbara Castle, the then Secretary of State.

79. The Main Entrance. No one who ever visited the old hutted hospital will ever forget the hissing pipes carrying the heating to the wards from the coal burning furnace!

80. Sidcup Cottage Hospital at the turn of the century. It had been built at the end of the 19th century, largely at the instigation of Dr. Shapley, and was closed in 1974 when the new Queen Mary's was opened. Situated in Granville Road, it has been replaced by the Sidcup Health Centre, a medical group practice.

Schools

81. Sidcup National School in Birkbeck Road was opened during the time of Rev. T. C. Lewis *(see illustration 34)*. One of the notable headmasters was Mr. Reuben Ashton who took over the boys' school in 1882 at the age of 23 and did not retire until 1919. His wife taught in the girls' school. Their son, Cyril, a captain in the Royal West Kent Regiment, died of his wounds on 12 March 1918 on the Western Front at 23 years of age. His father had been so proud of his entry to Dartford Grammar School through a scholarship. The family lived at 'Norton' in Church Avenue. The school became a county school in 1938 and in 1972 it moved to its present site in Alma Road. The old school has now become Doreen Bird's Dance School.

82. The present Birkbeck Primary School. This had been part of the Alma Road School for Girls before it amalgamated with the boys' school and moved to the new school premises in Bexley Lane, as Cleve Park School.

83. St Joseph's Convent in Hatherley Road, seen here during the First World War. It was run by a French order of nuns and a former pupil who attended in the 1930s reported that the nuns were lovely and that she enjoyed her time there. The girls were not allowed to mix with the boys. The uniform consisted of a navy blue drill slip reaching to the knees and a blazer with black buttons. In the winter they wore a hat and in the summer a white panama with a navy blue band. The school closed a few years ago as the order had to consolidate in France.

84. Children from Birkbeck National School dancing around the maypole in the vicarage garden of St John's in 1904.

85. Maypole dancing at Sidcup Hill School, *c*.1910. This was a county school opened in 1904. The teachers are Miss Woolmer and Mr. Cook. The old Ursula Lodges can be seen behind the trees.

86. The High School for Girls at the corner of Station and Victoria Road around 1914. The school later moved to Beaverwood on the other side of the Sidcup bypass. It is now the Sidcup Music Centre.

87. The rear of the High School for Girls. This garden is now a car park.

88. A classroom at the High School around 1914. It seems that two classes were being taught in the same room.

89. The gymnasium. This postcard, like that of the previous illustration, was printed in Berlin for a British company, the Photo Tourists Association of Turnham Green.

90. Rather a mystery photograph. It shows a group of school girls outside their school in the 1900s. The school board says 'School for Girls with Kindergarten'. It is believed to be Miss Perkins School for Girls in Hatherley Crescent.

91. Foots Cray National School in Church Road *c*.1900. It was first built in 1815 and patronised by Benjamin Harenc and Lord Bexley of Foots Cray Place. It was rebuilt in 1883. The marks made by pupils sharpening their slate pencils can still be seen on the wall by the school entrance. It is now a private preparatory school, 'The Harenc School'.

92. The second Lamorbey National School in Hurst Road. It was built in 1880 to replace the original in Burnt Oak Lane. It is now the Church Hall, a third school having been built near the Glade in 1969.

93. Some of 'The Hollies' children by the Burnt Oak Lane entrance in the 1900s. All the children were either orphans or those taken into care and were placed in cottages with house mothers and fathers.

94. A similar view of The Hollies without the children but showing the staff in the background. The practice of having house mothers and fathers was a model widely copied both nationally and internationally in the early years of this century.

95. 'Hollies' boys at work on the school garden at Burnt Oak Lane School. This was the school belonging to the Homes, but in 1936 it was taken over by the Kent Education Committee. The photograph was taken in the late 1920s.

96. Sidcup Hill School and a physical education class around 1920. The teacher is believed to be a Mr. Bechervaise.
The house in the background was formerly owned by a market garden. It is now in Middleton Avenue having been
swallowed up by 1930s building.

97. Staff at Blackfen Secondary School dressed up at the time of the Coronation of Queen Elizabeth II in 1953. Soon afterwards the boys' school was moved to Hurst Road and became Hurstmere School.

98. Hurstmere School under construction in Hurst Road in 1955-6. Its headmaster from 1946 until 1971 was J. W. Watts.

99. Two Hurstmere boys, David Perkins and Christopher Webb, contemplating a model of a Roman villa they have been building. This picture dates from 1958.

100. The boarded-up cottages at the Burnt Oak Lane entrance to The Hollies when the Homes were closed. Now they are refurbished for sale under a Conservation Development Area plan.

Foots Cray Then and Now

101. The farm cottage of Foots Cray Place. Now called 'Garden Cottage', it lies at the entrance to Foots Cray Meadows from Rectory Lane. The photograph was taken in Sir John Pender's time (1876-98), though the cottage dates back to Bourchier Cleve in 1754.

102. The pavilion in the grounds of Foots Cray Place. This was built to house a billiard room and other recreational pastimes for Lord Waring and his male guests. It was also where Lord Waring kept his mistress. Later it was let to the headmaster of Alma Road Boys' School (now Cleve Park). It is presently in a dilapidated state, although it will shortly be refurbished by a private buyer.

103. Foots Cray Lane (now Rectory Lane) in the inter-war years. All Saints church can be seen in the background and the farm cottage of Foots Cray Place lies to the left.

104. Foots Cray Lane further up the hill to Sidcup. This has hardly altered over the years and cars still have to take great care when negotiating the narrow road with its steep banks.

105. Another view of the farm cottage (see illustration 101) showing the neat paling fence that was built along the boundaries of Foots Cray Place. According to the Census of 1891 Alexander Baxter, born in Morayshire, was living here as a gardener with his wife and four children. Jessie Baxter, aged 16, was a pupil teacher at the local National School.

106. Foots Cray High Street in 1900 showing the *Seven Stars* on the right. The road is still narrow on account of the bridge over the Cray and because the public house is a listed building believed to be medieval in origin.

107. Foots Cray High Street looking towards the crossroads. Note the 'Tudor Cottages' on the left; only they and the *Red Lion* survive today. The buildings on the right have been replaced by a row of shops and a large supermarket.

108. The High Street looking east towards the *Seven Stars* and bridge, *c.*1928. The garden behind overlooks the River Cray and the site of the old papermill.

109. A policeman on point duty at the crossroads in the 1920s. Only Belgrave Terrace still remains (*see* illustration 25). It used to be called Catt's Corner after the name of the shopkeeper. To the left is Sidcup Hill and straight ahead lies the school and church and ultimately Foots Cray Meadows.

110. The King's Tea Gardens, Foots Cray, around 1900. This was a popular place for the locals and for those living in Eltham and Lewisham and beyond who came by bus for the day. A horse bus operated from London as early as 1845. Sidcup Garage was built on the site in 1924. In 1924 there were three No. 21 bus services. One every 12 minutes to Wood Green via London Bridge and two, two-hourly services, from Farningham to Sidcup Station and Wood Green to Farningham.

King's Tea Gardens, Foot's Cray.

111. Skating on the canal in Foots Cray Place. The River Cray was diverted to form a canal and lake for the residents of the big house to enjoy. Here can be seen guests (or servants?) preparing to skate. The laundry and north lodge can be seen in the background at the top right. The lake was drained during the Second World War and used as a rubbish tip, but now it has been grassed over though the outline of the waterway can still be traced.

ON THE MAIN TERRACE.

The Band of the Royal Regiment of Artillery.

By kind permission of

COL. E. H. A. WHITE, C.B., C.M.G., D.S.O., R.A.

And Officers of the Regiment.

WILL PLAY SELECTIONS DURING THE

1.	MARCHE	"L'Entente Cordiale" -	- *Allier*
2.	OVERTURE -	- "Mirella" -	- *Gounod*
3.	SUITE -	- "Coppélia" -	- *Delibes*
4.	SELECTION -	- "Tannhäuser"	- *Wagner*
5.	HUMORESKE -	- Moon Time"	- *Collins*
6.	INTERMEZZO	"The Mill in the Valley"	- *Rhodes*

CONDUCTOR : SGT. MAJOR, ELLIS.

PERFORMANCES WILL BE GIVEN BY

MARGARET MORRIS DANCERS 4.15—4.45

and

(Musical Accompaniment by the Band) 5.15 — 5.45

ON THE EAST LAWN.

MARGARET

AND

IN THE

SHOULD WEATH

112. A programme of entertainment devised by Lord Waring and held in Foots Cray Place in 1922.

113. The graves of the Birch family in Foots Cray churchyard. The Rev. Charles Birch was Rector of All Saints church from 1861 until 1910. It is probably his carriage which can be seen in illustration 26. When he died the headmistress, Miss Burrage, wrote in the school log book, 'It is with deep regret that I have to record the death of our beloved Rector, Rev. C. Birch, who expired suddenly on Sunday'. The school closed for the funeral.

M E.

ON THE BOWLING GREEN.

The Band of the 1st. Btn. Queen's Royal Regiment.

By kind permission of
LT.-COL. H. C. WHINFIELD
And Officers of the Regiment.

ON INCLUDING THE FOLLOWING :—

1. SYMPHONIC MARCH   -   -   -   - *Mancini*
2. OVERTURE   - " William Tell "   -   - *Rossini*
3. CELEBRATED HUNGARIAN DANCES   -   - *Brahms*
4. INTERMEZZO-HAWAIIAN
        " Malindas Fairy Bower "   - *Ord Hume*
5. FOX TROT   " Aint we got fun "   -   - *Whiting*
6. SONG   -   -   " Parted "   -   -   - *Tosti*

CONDUCTOR : Bandmaster J. BUCKLE.

DEMONSTRATION OF

MARCONI WIRELESS BROADCASTING
IN THE DINING SALOON.   5– 5.30 and 6—6.30.

DANCERS

ING

MARQUEE

VOURABLE.

114. The Runic Cross erected in All Saints churchyard to commemorate the Pender family. Sir John Pender, the pioneer of submarine telegraphy, lived in Foots Cray Place from 1876 to 1898. The cross was brought down in the 1987 hurricane and rebuilt by Cable and Wireless and English Heritage in 1993.

115. The last of the steam rollers hiding the shops and cottages pulled down to make way for Bertha Hollamby Court (sheltered accommodation). Taken in 1963, it catches the author's late wife with young daughter, in the foreground.

116. Meadow flowers once again flourish in Foots Cray Meadows, due mainly to sympathetic husbandry.

Sidcup Then and Now

117. The High Street looking west. The large vehicle is selling American lamp oil, i.e. paraffin. This is around 1900, so there are no cars. Note that the roof line has hardly changed over the years.

118. The High Street, looking east, with Alfred Dewey's shop on the extreme right, around the turn of the century.

119. The crossroads by the police station. What is now Barclays Bank appears to be a private house. Note the mucky state of the road and absence of traffic. This police station was opened in 1902 and so sets the date of the photograph around 1910.

120. The shop of S. H. Wright at the corner of Black Horse Road. He was a tradesman of many parts including an appraiser (property valuer), and undertakers (now carried on by Udens Ltd, High Street).

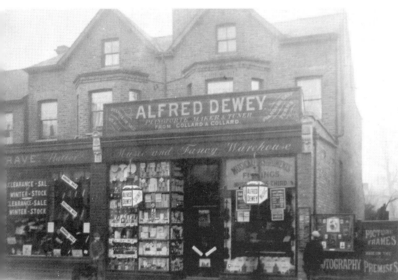

121. Alfred Dewey opened a music warehouse (where Fosters, the clothiers now stands). Although a tradesman, he occupied a prominent position locally and was a member of the Foots Cray Urban District Council and the Bromley Board of Guardians. He was a great beekeeper and photographer. He sold his business just before the First World War and retired to Wilmington.

122. Alfred Dewey's emporium in the High Street, just before the First World War. There is no longer a toy shop in Sidcup.

123. The High Street looking east before the First World War. This gives a good view of Dawson's, the department store, where Gateway can now be found. Up until at least 1960, Sidcup was virtually self-contained as a shopping centre.

124. A No.21 Tilling Stevens bus to Lewisham being driven in the direction of the police station just after the end of the First World War. St Lawrence's church can be seen on the left in the background.

125. The High Street from the *Black Horse* looking west. A No.11 bus approaching with two cars, 1930s.

126. Post Second World War Sidcup with Mence Smith and Cave Austins still very much in evidence. Hadlow Road is on the right just before the pillar box.

127. The High Street, just after the Second World War. The Regal Cinema does teas and the traffic is relatively light.

128. The crossroads with an early set of traffic lights. The large house on the corner of Elm Road has yet to be demolished and become successively Liptons and Blockbusters. Note the façade of Burton the tailors on the right.

129. Woolworth's was opened in 1934. Note the prices! A coach load of employees and families is going out for the day. Martin's Bank is to the left. This was taken around 1936, judging by the Oxford bags worn by the young man in the left front.

130. Robins Stores in the High Street in the late 1930s. No self-service then!

131. Close-up views of three shops in Clyde Terrace in 1910 with the blinds withdrawn. Williams sold boots and shoes, Walter Wade was a chemist and Stockwell was a stationer.

132. Hatherley Road. The postcard is postmarked 1905. This was a road of large houses built in the 1870s and '80s. Few have survived.

133. Shops at the corner of Hatherley Road. The corner shop is again a wine shop. This is Clyde terrace c.1910.

134. At the bottom of Hatherley Road are to be found these extravagantly built late-Victorian houses. There is a profusion of chevron and dogtooth ornamentation. They and the houses opposite are affectionately called 'The Old Ladies'.

135. Frognal Avenue in 1907. The lodge and coach house of Frognal House can be seen on the right of the picture.

136. Another view of Frognal Avenue (sometimes called Watery Lane). The wrought-iron gate remains but is in a poor condition.

137. The Green, Sidcup around 1896. The house, 'Freeby', home to Mrs. Marjorie Mills for so many years, is newly built. It still stands but is to be divided into flats.

138. This postcard bears the postmark 10 July 1907. It shows more of the Green, which in origin is part of Chislehurst Common. The Manor House lies to the left.

139. The Manor House today following its refurbishment as the Registry and Social Services Offices. It was built around 1790 on the site of an old farmhouse and was at first called Place Green House. It was renamed the Manor House in the 1860s though there never was a Manor of Sidcup. As well as being a private house, it has been a hospital and a school (The Manor House School, Miss Blofield, Headmistress).

140. The Blackfen Public Library in Holly Park. It was opened in 1936.

141. This is Crescent Road off Station Road. It has a number of large houses dating from the Victorian period and some built in the 1930s and post-war. The photograph shows the well-trimmed hedges of the house in Station Road.

142. Station Road looking down towards the station. Manor Road is to the left of the row of shops. All the trees and houses have been cleared and more shops and offices have been built since this picture was taken earlier this century.

143. Station approach to the left and Hatherley Crescent beyond the lamp post. From the look of the bus and the children's clothes this must have been taken in the 1920s.

144. Looking towards the railway station and bridge in Edwardian times (the postcard is dated 31 March 1909). The houses on the left have been demolished to make way for Marlowe House, and those on the right have given way to shops and offices.

145. Carlton Road was built in the 1870s as an estate for the new professionals who had moved to Sidcup because of the railway. Most of the houses which were designed and built by Hawkins have survived, although some have since been converted into flats. This is the best preserved area of Victoriana in the district and, together with the Green and much of Elm Road, it has been made a conservation area.

146. 'Westburton' in The Park, the street next to Carlton Road where James Turner, the author, lived as a child. The house has survived but has now been divided into a house and two flats.

147. A shop in Birkbeck Road around 1914. Extra houses and shops were required as the railway brought an influx of new residents. They were for the artisans and working class of new Sidcup.

148. The same shop and house next door in 1994. The shop has become a house with the front paved for car parking. Note the plaque on the wall of the next door house. It is also in the earlier picture. Who is it supposed to be?

149. The duck pond at the junction of Selborne Road and Rectory Lane. It was drained in the 1960s and some elegant neo-Georgian terraced houses were built over it.

150. Clare Terrace at the top of Sidcup Hill. Built in the 1880s, it has had a great variety of shop and business uses, and at one time the *Sidcup & District Times* printing press was based here. This photograph was taken in 1976.

151. Sidcup Hill in 1900. The house behind the fence on the right is still there but the houses opposite and all the way down the hill, with one exception, have been demolished to make way for much smaller properties. The terraced houses on the right behind the carts were built in the 1890s by one of the Knight family and still survive.

152. Durham Road built in the early 1900s off Sidcup Hill. The postcard is franked 14 September 1928 and says, 'If fine we will leave Sidcup at 2 o'clock, Love Esther'. It is addressed to Miss Haltreck, 179, Griffen Road, Plumstead SE18.

153. Floods in Willersley Avenue in 1968.

154. The Sidcup bypass soon after it was opened in the late 1920s. There are as many bicycles as motor vehicles!

155. The crossroads at Perry Street taken in the late 1940s. Compare this with the elaborate fly-overs now!

156. Main Road with Longlands Park Road just visible on the right by the row of shops. There seems to have been little change, apart from the volume of traffic, since this photograph was taken in the early '20s.

157. The house of Evans Nursery in Main Road. The nursery has moved to Ruxley but the interesting Victorian house remains.

WOODSIDE ROAD

158. Old Forge Way designed by Kenneth Dalgleish in 1936 in the style of 17th- and 18th-century cottages of the Kent and Sussex Weald. This was the first conservation area designated in Sidcup. They were built on the site of a large house called 'The Grange' where Mr. Tolhurst, a diamond merchant, once lived.

159. 'Maison Rouge', once the home of Dr. Frank Shapley. It was built in the 1880s and is now the United Services Club.

160. Memorial Card for
Dr. Shapley (*see* caption
62). His funeral took place
on Sunday, 19 November
1899 in St John's church.

St. John's Church, Sidcup.

❧ HYMNS ❧

TO BE SUNG AT THE

Funeral of Frank Shapley
(M.R.C.S.)

SUNDAY, NOV. 19th, 1899.

MY GOD, my FATHER, while I stray,
  Far from my home, on life's rough way
O teach me from my heart to say,
        " Thy Will be done."

Though dark my path, and sad my lot,
Let me be still and murmur not,
Or breathe the prayer divinely taught,
        " Thy Will be done."

What though in lonely grief I sigh
For friends beloved no longer nigh
Submissive would I still reply,
        " Thy Will be done."

If Thou shouldst call me to resign
What most I prize, it ne'er was mine ;
I only yield Thee what is Thine ;
        " Thy Will be done."

Let but my fainting heart be blest
With Thy sweet SPIRIT for its guest,
My GOD, to Thee I leave the rest ;
        " Thy Will be done."

Renew my will from day to day,
Blend it with Thine, and take away
All that now makes it hard to say,
        " Thy Will be done."   Amen.

161. The Scouts and Cubs on the vicarage lawn around 1928. In the first row seated are Canon E. B. Spurgin (fourth from the left), Roy Shapley (fourth from the right) and Victor Plant (third from the right).

162. The Rover Scouts on the vicarage lawn in 1928. Leighton Spurgin, the vicar's son, is seated second from right in the front row and next to him (third from right) is Roy Shapley.

Halfway Street, Lamorbey and Blackfen

163. The shops on the right of Station Road under the bridge. Hurst Road is behind the trees. This photograph dates from 1910 and shows change only in the shop names and trades.

164. A policeman posing for his picture at the corner of Hurst Road and Penhill Road.

165. Halfway Street where the sorting office now stands. These were called Church Cottages.

166. This view, *c*.1907, shows the same side of the street as illustration 165, but taken from across the road and showing Lamorbey House (sometimes known as Halfway Street House). The Drill Hall was built on the site which in turn has been taken over by British Telecom.

167. The *Olde Black Horse* and Lamorbey Stores further along from Lamorbey House. The pub survives.

168. The Limes, Halfway Street seen from the rear. S. H. Butcher Esq. Chevalier de l'ordre de la Couronne de Belgique lived here in the early years of this century. It has been preserved in the Conservation Area.

169. Cottages opposite the main entrance to The Hollies rejoicing in such names as Primrose Cottage, Acacia Cottage and Westbrook Cottage. Wingfield Place was to the rear. This picture dates from *c*.1912

170. The village, Halfway Street, *c*.1910, showing the post office, Jessamine Cottage, Rose Cottage and Elmleigh.

171. The more substantial cottages opposite to Burnt Oak Lane and near to the 'Tudor Cottage'. This picture was taken around the turn of the century.

172. This is the site of the Old Red House where Miss Beamish lived until her death some fifty years ago. She left her land to The Hollies but the authority did not want to extend further so the property decayed. When the Home closed and the land was freed for development, it was subject to several attempts to build, but the developers were not able to construct to the satisfaction of the standards of the Conservation Area. This view shows the acceptable development which was completed in 1993.

173. 8 Burnt Oak Lane, Lamorbey, was built in 1841. This was formerly known as 'Mrs. Malcolm's School' where children who lived on the Lamorbey Estate were taught.

174. Burnt Oak Lane around 1900 looking towards Halfway Street. The site of the future Burnt Oak Lane School is on the right. The cottages on the left were built by the Malcolms for their estate workers in 1870 and are still there, having recently been restored.

175. A bridge across the Wyncham or the Shuttle. The postmark on the card is 30 March 1907, and reads, 'This is a bridge near us. We have been having lovely weather and the country looks very nice. I hope you are having as good weather at Girton. Best wishes for Easter from M. K. Pillman'. It was addressed to Mrs. Palmer at Girton College, Cambridge. The Pillmans lived at Craybank, Foots Cray and were on the telephone (Sidcup 354).

176. M. J. Sims, post office and newsagent, Halfway Street in 1957.

177. Halfway Street just past The Hollies entrance on the right. About 1920.

178. Map of Montrose Park Estate in 1933, showing development intended for Hurst Road, Canterbury Avenue, Chaucer Road and Foots Cray Lane. The houses on the right of Foots Cray Lane were never built as part of the Montrose Park Estate.

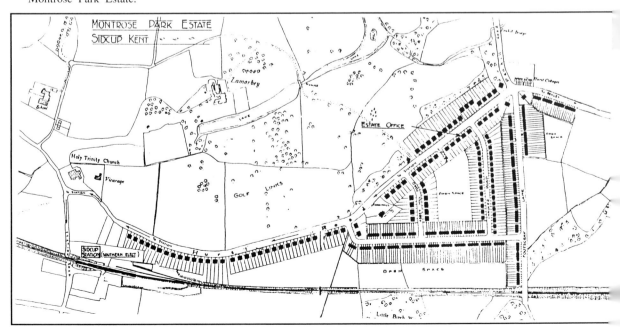

179. The Oval, soon after it was built in 1935. There has been little change since then. This, too, is a Conservation Area, as it encapsulates the style of the 1930s.

180. The Woodman, Blackfen, in the 1930s. It was built by Kenneth Dalgleish in 1931 to look like a much older building.

181. Days Lane, Sidcup, developed in the 1930s and named after Day's Farm. Holy Redeemer and Days Lane Baptist churches are located along this road.

North Cray

182. The Almshouses were built by the Rev. Hetherington of North Cray Place in the 1770s. They stood opposite the Dower House in North Cray Road and were demolished to make way for the dual carriageway in the 1970s.

183. The lodge at North Cray Place now cut off on both sides by the dual carriageway and the old road leading to the church of St James. Taken in the early 1970s.